Outrage for dharma

Pass on the heritage of resistance

S. Kalyanaraman

ISBN: 0982897138
ISBN-13: 978-0-9828971-3-3

Library of Congress Control Number (LCCN): 2012901762

Sarasvati Research Center, Herndon, VA

DEDICATION

The Outrage for Dharma is dedicated to all people of the globe who are destined to seize power into their own hands to create a Rastram for Dharma.

CONTENTS

(let noble thoughts come to us from all sides)

ACKNOWLEDGMENTS

Many savants have fought for the liberties many people of the globe enjoy today. Liberty given to us by our ancestors is a treasure which has to be preserved by a determined population of the globe. The preservation of liberty and non-violent resistance are a treasure, a heritage handed down to us by our ancestors. Deploy this treasure. The outrage for dharma is a crying out derived from many warriors of past eras.

1 WHY SHOULD THERE BE OUTRAGE FOR DHARMA?

Dharma is philosophia *perennis*, et *universalis*. This global ethic is eternal, inviolate.

The recurrence of the outrage for dharma is independent of epochs, is an affirmation of consciousness; and a declaration of universal truths of the nature of reality and humanity.

There should be an outrage, a crying out for dharma because many evil forces have taken hold of the state. State which should only be an instrument for protecting dharma has become selfish, insolent and brutal. It is time to halt this aberrant situation when the state players have become votaries of adharma, a negation of everything dharma stands for.

It is time to recall the past role models of resistance. It is time to pass on the heritage of resistance.

It is time to choose the non-violent resistance model to restore the state back to its subordinate role as a servant of the people, a mere instrument to exercise peoples' power for the benefit of the people.

Our ancestors cried out and led us towards justice and freedom.

Now is the time for you to follow this heritage, to cry out and lead us towards justice and freedom. Freedom to be. Freedom to cherish the divine blessing of dharma and to gain the strength to protect dharma for a just order of social welfare.

2 WHAT IS DHARMA?

In an ancient text called *Bhagavadgita* (Song divine), a reference is made to two types of paths: the path of knowledge and the path of action. Explaining this, Adi Shankara in his *Gita Bhashyam* notes: "Dharma is verily two-fold, characterized by social action (*pravritti*) and inward contemplation (*nivritti*), designed to promote order in this world. This two-fold dharma aims at true social welfare and emancipation of all beings."

Dharma is thus defined as the order in the world which promotes social welfare and leads to emancipation (absolute bliss or cessation of pain) of all beings.

That which leads to the attainment of *abhyudayam* (prosperity in this world) and *nihśreyas* (total cessation of pain and attainment of eternal bliss) is Dharma. (*Vaiśeṣika sutra* 1.11-12).

In what is perhaps the oldest human document, Rigveda defines social action (*pravritti* which is elaborated in three facets: righteousness, prosperity and desire): Upon such action rests the whole manifest universe with its mobile life-form (*ātman*) and immobile forms and phenomena (*dhātu*). On the other hand, *nivritti* is that which leads one to the unmanifest and the eternal divine. The Sanskrit text reads: (RV 1.022.18): *trīṇi padā vicakrame viṣṇu gopā adābhyah ato dharmāṇi dhārayan* (Trans. 'The preserver of all the worlds, the uninjurable took three steps, upholding thereby righteous acts.)

Mahanarayanopanishad (Section 79.7) declares thus:

> *dharmo viśvasya jagatah pratiṣṭā*
> *loke dharmiṣṭa prajā upasarpanti*
> *dharmeṇa pāpamapanudati*
> *dharme sarvam pratiṣṭitam*
> *tasmāddharmam paramam vadanti*

Dharma constitutes the foundation of all affairs in the world. People respect those who adhere to Dharma. Dharma insulates (man) against sinful thoughts. Everything in this world is founded on Dharma. Dharma, therefore, is considered supreme.

Dharma is that which exalts and bestows the Supreme Good or Absolute Bliss (cessation of pain).

The globe is upheld by Dharma. (*Prthivīm dharmaṇā dhṛtam – Atharva Veda*). This upholding is depicted as a sculptural metaphor.

In ever-changing phenomena of the worlds, three aspects of change are identified by Patañjali Sutra (3.13):

1. Transformation of a thing (dharma) into a property (dharma);
2. Transformation of a property into a mark (lakṣaṇa); and
3. Transformation of a mark into a condition (avasthā).

Change applies to both physical substance (*bhūta*) and sensations (*indriya*).

3 DHARMA IN ACTION

Dharma is a set of dynamic principles.

Dharma is a set of ordering principles.

There can be specific attributes of dharma specific in time and space. The attributes are related to the competences, proclivities and preferences of groups of individuals with their own circles of affection and interaction. This is why Rigveda notes the emergence of the first dharma-s in the first *yajña* (oblation, sacred offering) of Prajāpati: *tāni dharmāni prathamāni āsan.*

.

Sanatana Dharma (eternal ordering principle)
Sāmānya Dharma (common principle)

Viśeṣa Dharma (special principle)
Varṇāśrama Dharma or Kula dharma (kula – family lineage and social Order)
Svadharma (Dharmacarth = dharma carati = nature (Thai) = Responsibility, according to one's nature.
Yuga Dharma (principles relevant for the age or period in history)
Mānava Dharma (human responsibility)
Rāja Dharma (king's responsibility)
Pravritti Dharma (righteous conduct for outer -- worldly life)
Nivritti Dharma (righteous conduct for inner—spiritual life)

4 DHARMA-DHAMMA

Dharma as a principle of motion, of tradition (*paramparā*): Dharma is recognized in Jaina, Bauddham continuum.

Gautama, the Buddha, refers to *eṣa dhammo sanantaṇo*, this dharma eternal. He explains *dhamma* as "dependently arisen phenomena" (*paticca-samuppanna-dhamma*). In addition to signifying the overarching ethical order, the quintessential functions of a given profession (say, of artisans or merchants or soldiers) are signified by the word '*dharma*': (e.g. *kṣatriya dharma, vaiśya dharma,* etc), the *dharma* of relationships (e.g., *āśrama dharma* 'responsibilities inherent in a particular stage of life'). Thus *dharma* binds a community to discipline, highlighting social responsibility.

In the Jaina thought, dharma and adharma are defined as the principle of motion and principle of rest. The two phenomena are said to pervade the whole of *loka-ākāśa* 'universal space'; they are subtle; movement is associated with either a *jīva* or pudgala (being *sakriya dravya-s*, 'flows of action'); the movement is dependent upon the presence of dharma.

Dharma dravya makes movement possible; an analogy is provided by fish swimming, noting that swimming is impossible without the presence of water.

Adharma dravya enables a moving object, living or non-living to come to rest. The analogy is of a bird coming to a stop by ceasing to beat its wings; this is contingent upon the bird ceasing to fly perching on a tree branch or on the ground. The two principles, dharma and adharma account for the definite structure of the world. So, too, *kāla* 'time', is a *dravya* – movement, a motion from being to becoming.

In Bauddham: *anussava itiha-itiha-paramparā-piṭaka-sampadā dhamma* – Dharma is a system of moral discipline which is based upon customs, usages, or traditions handed down from time immemorial. (*Majjhima-nikāya*, I.520).

5 METAPHORS OF COSMIC ORDER

Many metaphors were deeloped by our ancestors to convey the essence of cosmic order.

Created as a constant reminder of a greater cosmic order, Angkor Wat shows several apparent solar alignments with a nearby mountaintop shrine. A person standing at Pre Rup, six kilometers away, could watch the sun set over Angkor Wat at winter solstice. A person standing in the southwestern corner of the temple could watch a rising sun through the eastern gate during the summer solstice. Space Imaging's IKONOS satellite took this image of Angkor Wat April 12, 2004. Photo credit: Space Imaging http://www.spaceimaging.com/gallery/ancientobservatories/

Cosmic dancer: *cakra* – cyclical motion as a continuum -- as a metaphor of dharma (A sculptural fragment in Patna Museum).

A Jaina cosmic diagram, Gujarat, c.1500. "Gujarat, circa 16th Century. The circular diagram flanked by a pair of eyes and centered at top with the sacred syllables: 'Ohm' and 'Hrim', painted with a white-clad Swetambara figure surrounded by lotus petals and the 24 tirthankara-s with two twenty-armed female divinities and two four-armed female divinities at the corners and numerous divinities arranged in registers, richly gilt and painted on a red ground with inscriptions in Devanāgari around the central figure 28¾ x 24 in. (73 x 61 cm.)."

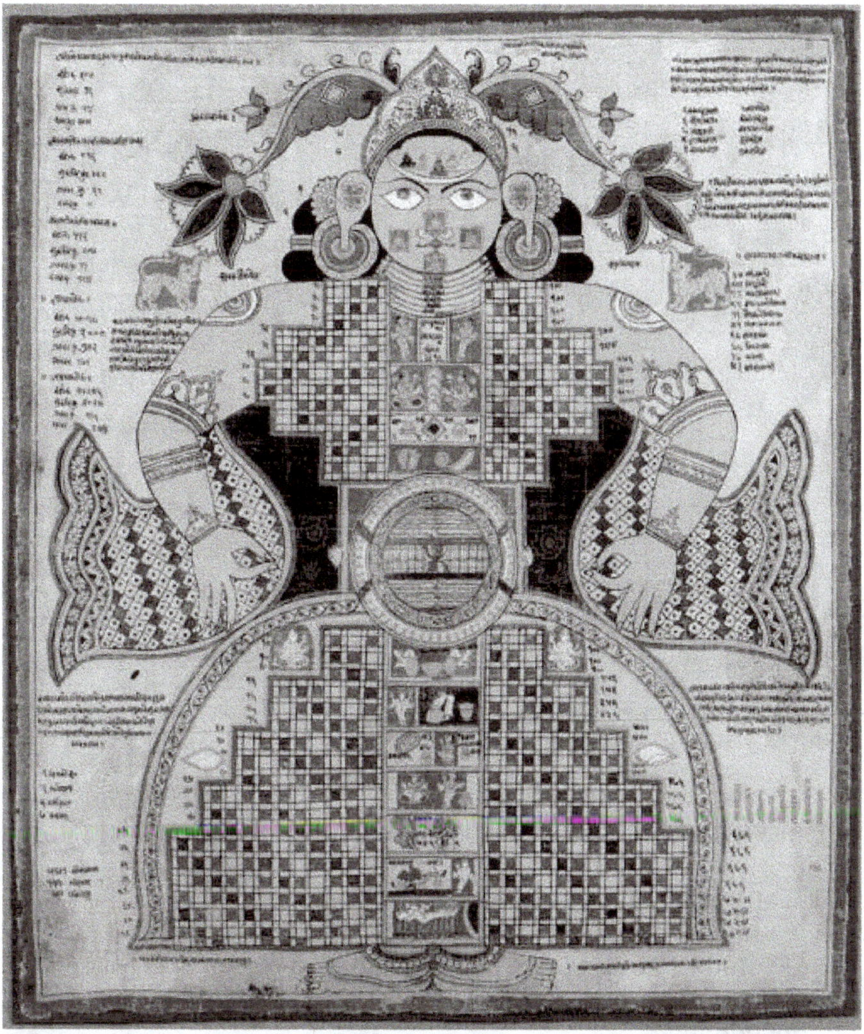

A "purushkara yantra," a diagram based on a cosmic human figure, 18th Century. Depicting a Cosmic figure with flaring sashes in a grid pattern of red and green squares with the circular Middle World *Jambudvīpa* at center, seven levels of hell in area of legs, and the heavens in the upper body with 8 Jinas painted in the face, the outer space decorated with elephants, conches and dancing female divinities, framed 34 x 30 in.

6 ORDERING THE TERRESTRIAL WORLD

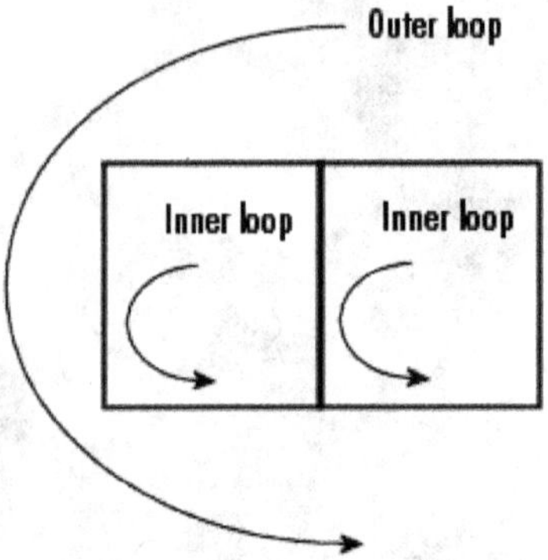

Inner space - Outer space

Degrees of freedom

If the angular velocities along a closed loop cannot be made consistent, the driveline is over-constrained and cannot move.

To achieve dharma as movement, to move towards *abhyudayam*, the closed loops – *pravritti, nivritti* -- have to be made consistent.

Deviations from dharma have to be rectified.

- Premise: Movement is needed to realize human potential, *nihśreyas* (sāmānya dharma, 'ethic'), social capital, *abhyudayam*
- Harmonise the quest for inner peace (inner space) and abhyudayam – general welfare, *loka hitam* -- of social order (outer space)
- Re-establish the primacy of human responsibility and duties (juxtaposed to Human rights) : Rights flow from performance of duties (vratam, vratā 'law')
- Re-establish the freedom to enquire (different pantha-s, realizing that cosmic order is knowable)
- Dharma is celebration of freedom, freedom to move from Being to Becoming

7 RASTRAM IS ORGANIZING FOR DHARMA

The concept of rastram is elucidated in the context of dharman and ṛta. *asṛgam indavah pathā dharmann rtasya suśriyah*

(Trans. With the support of and along ṛta, the principle of truth and order, flow essences; dharman stands parallel to *pathā*, 'path'.) (RV 9.7.1)

What is this path? The answer is provided by the derivation of the word, 'rāṣṭram'. The root is raj, 'to be resplendent, shine'. (*Dhātup.* Xix, 74). Soma and Varuna are raja, 'guidance'. (RV 10.49.4). Rāṣṭram is the mover in the path.

Derivation: *rāj dīptau sthaa gatinivrttau*, 'when the path is lost, the rāṣṭram provides the light.' (rāj, rājita 'shine , glitter'). rāj (Vedic also *rāṣṭi*) 'anything the best or chief of its kind' as in: *śankharāj*, 'best śankhā (*turbinella pyrum*) conch'. Rj 'to go ; to stand or be firm ; to obtain , acquire ; to be strong or healthy.' This is why Vāk Devi says she is the *rāstrī samgamanī*, 'moving in splendor'. She, rāstrī, constitutes the stability for a group of people and phenomena. She moves firmly and resolutely; she is *śakti*.

Rāstrī is 'proprietress', the possessor of all resplendence. Rāstrī is divine genitrix, Devi, uniting people for abhyudayam. Calling herself rāstrī , she says: *aham* rāstrī *samgamanī vasūnām*, I am the Rastram uniting and moving people for creating wealth. (RV 10.125) There cannot be a more emphatic and precise definition of the Rastram which was founded on dharma, the global ethic. *rāstram vai aśvamedhah*, trans. 'building up of the nation is *aśvamedha*'. The exhortation is to build the nation with valor (*aśva*) and intellect (*medha*). [*śathapathabrāhmaṇa* (13.1.6.3)]

Rāstrī, rastram have to be distinguished from the commonly used terms, 'nation', and 'state' which are mere groupings for governance. 'Nation' is a concept still unresolved as seen from the dissolution of the state of Union of Soviet Socialist Republic (USSR).

Rastram is not a territorial construct but signifies a path, a road-map, in a polity, to enshrine dharma.

Rastram is founded on *ādhyatmika* foundations from the Rigveda and is governed by the active terms, samgam, samgamanī –united movements of people towards *abhyudayam*. Thus, Rastram is not a restricted construct related to a common language or territory but a common zeal to achieve welfare of people through united actions.

Rastram is the path which led our ancestors move into Europe, into Americas and across the Indian Ocean region to present the realization of janapada-s (community republics) and organization of the state or nation, governed by dharma, the global ethic.

History blends into the lives of every ordinary Indian positing Sri Rama and Sri Krsna as role-models in polity to protect dharma. Valmiki who wrote the story of Rama in *Rāmāyaṇa* calls Rama, vigrahavān dharmah (dharma personified). Vyasa who wrote the story of Krsna in Mahabharata depicts Krsna as the Gitacharya, teaching the world the basic tenets of dharma in action.

Sri Rama and Sri Krsna are engaged in the struggles of the rastram, harsh tests of life and time, to establish and sustain dharma. *Rāmāyaṇa* and *Mahābhārata* are *itihāsa*, 'narrative of happenings'. Yaska (11:25) notes that *Aitihāsika* explains Vedic thought while commenting upon *pāramparika katha* (traditional narratives). Thus, *itihāsa* teaches philosophy of life supported by historical evidence.

Sri Rama and his *vānara sena* led by the architects Nala and Nīla accomplish the historic feat of constructing Setubandha to provide a bridge across Setusamudram between India and Sri Lanka. The objective was to rescue Sita devi held captive by Ravana in a blatant act of adharma. Sita's rescue from captivity is dharmic action, *par excellence*, narrated in the *itihāsa, Rāmāyaṇa*. Rama is *maryāda puruṣottama*, the perfect among men, leading a life of self-control and virtue governed by the global ethic, dharma. He is *vigrahavān dharmah*, the embodiment of dharma.

Sri Kṛṣṇa and his associates Pāṇḍava-s involve the entire nation of Bharatam in the Great War fought to restore fairness and justice in the polity. Pāṇḍava-s were denied a fair share of the land by Kauravas and the war ensues. Sri Kṛṣṇa was the strategist who defeated the adharmic Kauravas in battle and presented the imperative of *dharmakṣetra* in *kurukṣetra*. *Dharmakṣetra* is the *punyabhumi* Bharat, the Mahābhārat, which has many *tirthasthāna*-s, 'sacred places' for all pilgrims of the world to travel offering prayers to *pitṛ*-s, ancestors who have given us our identity.

अहम् राष्ट्री संगमनी वसूनां चिकितुषी प्रथमा यग्नियानां , RV 10.125.03 I am the sovereign queen, the collectress of treasures, cognizant (of the Supreme Being), the chief of objects of worship; as such the divinities have put me in many places, abiding in manifold conditions, entering into numerous (forms.)

Rāṣṭram is a benediction (*anugraham*) and attributes of Rāṣṭram are defined in repetitive poetic refrain: *Vājasneyi Samhitā* 10.2-4:

वृष्णऽऊर्मिरसि राष्ट्रदा राष्ट्रम्मे देहि स्वाहा वृष्णऽऊर्मिरसि राष्ट्रदा राष्ट्रममुष्मै देहि

वृषसेनोसि राष्ट्रदा राष्ट्रममुष्मै देह्यर्थेत स्थ ।

अर्थेत स्थ राष्ट्रदा राष्ट्रम्मे दत्त स्वाहार्थेत स्थ राष्ट्रदा राष्ट्रमुष्मै दत्तोजस्वती स्थ राष्ट्रदा राष्ट्रम्मे दत्त स्वाहौजस्वती स्थ राष्ट्रदा राष्ट्रममुष्मै दत्ताप-:-
परिवाहिणी स्थ राष्ट्रदा राष्ट्रम्मे दत्त स्वाहाप-:-
परिवाहिणी स्थ राष्ट्रदा राष्ट्रममुष्मै दत्तापाम्पतिरसि

राष्ट्रदा राष्ट्रम्मे देहि स्वाहापाम्पतिरसि राष्ट्रदा राष्ट्रममुष्मै देह्यपाङ्गर्भोसि

राष्ट्रदा राष्ट्रममुष्मै स्वाहापाङ्गर्भोसि राष्ट्रदा राष्ट्रममुष्मै देहि सूर्यत्वचस स्थ ।

सूर्यत्वचस स्थ राष्ट्रदा राष्ट्रम्मे दत्त स्वाहा सूर्यत्वचस स्थ

राष्ट्रदा राष्ट्रममुष्मै दत्त स्वाहा सूर्यत्वचस स्थराष्ट्रदा राष्ट्रम्मे दत्त स्वाहा सूर्य त्वचस स्थ

राष्ट्रदा राष्ट्रममुष्मै दत्त मान्दा स्थ राष्ट्रदा राष्ट्रम्मे दत्त स्वाहा मान्दा स्थ

राष्ट्रदा राष्ट्रममुष्मै दत्त व्रजक्षित स्थ राष्ट्रदा राष्ट्रम्मे दत्त स्वाहा व्रजक्षित स्थ

राष्ट्रदा राष्ट्रममुष्मै दत्त वाशा स्थ राष्ट्रदा राष्ट्रम्मे दत्त स्वाहा वाशा स्थ

राष्ट्रदा राष्ट्रममुष्मै दत्त शविष्ठा स्थ राष्ट्रदा राष्ट्रम्मे दत्त शक्वरी स्थ

राष्ट्रदा राष्ट्रममुष्मै दत्त स्वाहा शक्वरी स्थ राष्ट्रदा राष्ट्रम्मे दत्त जनभृतं स्थ

राष्ट्रदा राष्ट्रममुष्मैदत्त स्वाहा जनभृतं स्थ राष्ट्रदा राष्ट्रम्मे दत्त विश्वभृतं स्थ

राष्ट्रदा राष्ट्रममुष्मैदत्त स्वाहा विश्वभृतं स्थ राष्ट्रदा राष्ट्रम्मे दत्ताप-:-
स्वराज स्थ राष्ट्रदा राष्ट्रममुष्मै दत्त ।

मधुमतीर्मधुमतीभिँ पृच्यन्ताम्महि क्षत्रङ्क्षत्रियाय वन्वानाऽअनाधृष्टाँ

सीदत सहौजसो महि क्षत्रङ्क्षत्रियाय दधतीँ ।

Vṛṣṇa ūrmirasi Rāṣṭradā Rāṣṭram me dehi svāhā Vṛṣṇa ūrmirasi Rāṣṭradā Rāṣṭramumuṣmai dehi

Vṛṣa senosi Rāṣṭradā Rāṣṭramumuṣmai dehi artheta stha

artheta stha Rāṣṭradā Rāṣṭram me datta svāhārtheta Rāṣṭradā Rāṣṭramumuṣmai dattojasvatī

stha Rāṣṭradā Rāṣṭram me datta svāhāpah

parivāhiṇī stha Rāṣṭradā Rāṣṭram me datta svāhāpah

parivāhiṇī stha Rāṣṭradā Rāṣṭramumuṣmai dattāpāmpatirasi

Rāṣṭradā Rāṣṭram me dehi svāhāmāmpatirasi Rāṣṭradā Rāṣṭramumuṣmai dehi apāngarbhosi

Rāṣṭradā Rāṣṭramumuṣmai dehi sūryatvacasa stha

sūryatvacasa stha Rāṣṭradā Rāṣṭram me datta svāhā sūryatvacasa stha

Rāṣṭramumuṣmai datta māndā stha Rāṣṭradā Rāṣṭram me datta svāhā vrajakṣita stha

Rāṣṭradā Rāṣṭramumuṣmai datta vāśā stha Rāṣṭradā Rāṣṭram me datta svāhā vāśā stha

Rāṣṭradā Rāṣṭramumuṣmai datta śaviṣṭhā stha Rāṣṭradā Rāṣṭram me datta śakvarī stha

Rāṣṭradā Rāṣṭramumuṣmai datta svāhā śakvarī stha Rāṣṭradā Rāṣṭram me datta janabhṛtam stha

Rāṣṭradā Rāṣṭramumuṣmai datta svāhā janabhṛtam stha Rāṣṭradā Rāṣṭram me datta viśvabhṛtam stha

Rāṣṭradā Rāṣṭramumuṣmai datta svāhā viśvabhṛtam stha Rāṣṭradā Rāṣṭram me dattāpah

Svarāja stha Rāṣṭradā Rāṣṭramumuṣmai datta

Madhumatīrmadhumatībhim pṛcyantāmmahi kṣatrankṣatriyāya vanvānā anādhṛṣṭām

Sīdata sahaujaso mahi kṣatrankṣatriyāya dadhatīm

These verses talk about many concepts which throw light on the grouping of Rāṣṭram, as a path for the supporters of people (*janabhṛta*) and supporters of the world (*viśvabhṛta*) and about the concept of self-rule (*svarāja*).

The divinities drew waters with their store of sweetness, succulent and observant, king-creating,
Wherewith they sprinkled Varuna and Mitra, wherewith they guided Indra past his foemen.
Wave of the male art thou, giver of kingship. Do thou—All-hail!—bestow on me the kingdom.
Wave of the male art thou, giver of kingship. Do thou on So-and-So bestow the kingdom.
Thou hast a host of males, giver of kingship. Do thou—All-hail!—bestow on me the kingdom.

A host of males hast thou, giver of kingship. Do thou on
So-and-So bestow the kingdom.
Swift at your work are ye, givers of kingship. Do ye—
All-hail!—bestow on me the kingdom.
Swift at your work are ye, givers of kingship. Do ye on
So-and-So bestow the kingdom.
Endowed with strength are ye, givers of kingship, etc.
O'erflowing floods are ye, etc.
The Waters' Lord art thou, giver of kingship. Do thou, etc.
The Waters' Child art thou, etc.
With sun-bright skins are ye, givers, etc.
Brilliant as Suns are ye, etc.
Bringers of joy are ye, etc.
Dwellers in cloud are ye, etc
Desirable are ye, etc.
Most powerful are ye, etc.
Endowed with might are ye, etc.
Man-nourishing are ye, etc.
All-nourishing are ye, etc.
Self-ruling Waters are ye, giving kingship. On So-and-So
do ye bestow the kingdom.
Together with the sweet let sweet ones mingle, obtaining
for the Kṣatriya mighty power.
Rest in your place inviolate and potent, bestowing on the
Kṣatriya mighty power.

The phrase: *Rāṣṭramumuṣmai dattojasvatī* is an invocation to bestow a Rāṣṭram with vigor, energy, ability, power – *ojas* – with vital warmth, light, splendor, lustre and a manifestation of action throughout the body politic. *Rāṣṭrī* is, in feminine form, the child of the waters.

Rāṣṭrī, Rāṣṭram, is a lustrous body politic of federating united states of people living along the Pacific, Atlantic, Indian Ocean waters. The nation is the nation of the people (gaṇa). A क्षत्रिय kṣatriya is endowed with sovereignty, and is a reigning, governing order.

Bhadram icchanta riṣayah swarvidah tapo dīkṣam upaniṣeduṣ agre
tato rāṣtram balam ojaśca jātam tadasmai devah upasannamantu

> The sages, aspiring for a higher and better standard, work with diligence and devotion; they inspire people to do their duty with dedication. This is the way how rashtram and communities grow strong. (*Atharva Veda* 19.41.1)

Brahmacaryena tapasā rājā rāṣtram virakṣati
Acharyo brahmacaryena brahmacarinamichhati

> By brahmacarya and tapas, rastram is protected. By brahmacarya acharya adores brahmacari. (Brahmacarya is action inspired by the divine. Brahmacaryam is parameṣṭyam, evocation of parameśwara.) (*Atharva Veda* 2.5.17).

The centrality of elders to declare dharma, *pitr*-s finds mention in a passage of *Mahābhārata*: *na sa sabha yatra na santi vrddha, nate vrddha ye na vadanti dharmam*. That is, an assembly where there are elders – the elders who declare dharma. Purohita, those in the front lines, were *rāṣṭragopa* (protectors of the realm).

8 SOMETHING IS ROTTEN IN THE STATE

After centuries of struggle, state as a social formation was recognized as a means to attain social welfare.

Many millions of human lives were sacrificed and enormous sufferings were tolerated by the people during this struggle.

The hard-won freedom and justice have now been endangered by the state, within a territorial domain of a nation, which has grown beyond its levels of incompetence, with many state operatives in collusion with corrupt renegades have lost allegiance to the oaths they took to serve the people by the rule of law.

Many state operatives have become selfish and insolent.

Money which is only a medium of social exchange has been transformed into a commodity and amassing wealth by illegal means has become an end in itself for most of the state operatives.

Spurious forms of money have been engineered calling them financial derivatives and hedge operations as insurance cover, while in fact using such instruments for speculative transactions governed by greed, impoverishing millions of people and looting nature's gifts.

Corporate forms which were earlier designed with in-built social responsibility mechanism of *śreṇi-dharma* (corporate ethic) setting apart a fixed percentage of their earnings for social causes have been mutilated to become corrupt instruments of power and pelf.

All societies attach importance to ethical values, *ātman* (innate cosmic energy) as also to the creation of wealth of a nation. An ascetic is as respected in society as a just ruler of a state. This remarkable integration of materialistic ethos with the social ethic is unique in the story of human civilizations.

Śreṇi dharma as social capital can supply the missing element of trusteeship.

Dharma refers to laws and also to fundamental duties or responsibilities governed by global ethic, leading to righteous conduct, and performance of righteous duty. The root of the word is *dhṛ* meaning 'that which upholds or supports', and is generally translated into English as the "law". Clearly stipulated rules of ethical behavior are exemplified by the directive in a Vedic text, the *Bṛhadāraṇyaka Upaniṣad*: *datta*, 'give' !

It is only after ethical rules (*yama* and *niyama*) are followed, *ātmajñāna* or self-realization (*nihśreyas*) can be attained. *nihśreyas* and *abhyudayam* (social welfare) constitute the twin facets of *dharma* , the inviolate, universal, eternal ethic.

astāṅga-yoga of Patañjali (2.29) emphasizes that ethical behavior is the foundation which leads to self-realization, *ātmajñāna* – realizing [*ahaṃ brahma-asmi* (*Bṛhadāraṇyaka Upaniṣad* I.4.10) trans. 'I am brahman, the supreme *ātman'; yas tu sarvāṇi bhūtāny-ātmany-eva-anupaśyati sarvabhūteṣu ca-ātmānam* (*Īśā Upaniṣad* 6) 'who sees all beings in oneself and oneself in all beings'.]

Yoga was a popular form in ancient regions of Asia and Europe, its foundations were based on rules of ethical behavior. Ethical behavior and self-realization were complementary, inseparable, and hence, the following eight stages (limbs) of Yoga are enunciated:

8) *samādhi* absorption
7) *dhyāna* meditation
6) *dhāraṇā* concentration of the mind

5) *pratyāhāra* withdrawal of the senses
4) *prāṇāyāma* breath regulation
3) *āsana* body position
2) *niyama* internal rules
1) *yama* external rules (code of conduct)

yama (1) and *niyama* (2) (external and internal rules of conduct): ethical behavior – yama and niyama – were the firm, first steps, fundamental and involved: *dharma, sukṛtāni, dāna.* [righteous duty, good deeds, liberality.]

Thus, without the first steps of social ethic, no self-realization is attainable through subsequent steps. The external rules of conduct, *yama*, are: *ahiṃsā satya asteya brahmacarya aparigraha* [non-injury; truth; non-stealing; life of purity; non-grabbing; non-amassing.]

Patañjali notes: *yogaś citta-vṛtti-nirodha;* trans. yoga effects the cessation of mind-movements. All such movements of thinking and feeling are caused by 5 *kleśas* ('negative human afflictions'). These are: *avidyā asmitā rāga dveṣa abhiniveśa* [ignorance; egoism (separate ego); attachment; passion; abhorrence; attachment to the world.]

We will begin discussion with philosophical underpinnings and then discuss practical aspects in the context of corporate behavior. The philosophical underpinning for trusteeship, as the statutory framework to set apart a pre-determined percentage of wealth for social causes, is derived from the injunction of an ancient sacred text, against excessive accumulation of wealth:

yāvad bhriyeta jaṭharam tāvat svatvam hi dehinām
adhikam yo 'bhimanyeta sa steno daṇḍam arhati

"One may claim proprietorship to as much wealth as required to maintain body and soul together, but one who desires proprietorship over more than that must be considered a thief, and he deserves to be punished by the laws of nature." (*Bhāgavatam* 7.14.8)

This stunning definition of proprietorship is the defining *dharma* for a corporation in ancient traditions which produced the *śreṇi dharma* . We are not suggesting that property ownership laws should be done away with. For example, the house belongs to the owner as his or her property but its *use* is constrained by social responsibility of the owner as a member of a *śreṇi,* a social corporation.

Corporate models of both capitalism and socialism operate within the framework of 'rational, materialistic economic ethos' premised on 'rational self-interest' of an individual, endeavoring to make the best choices with the available information. The corporate model of *śreṇi dharma* is a paradigm shift – taking the rational individual self-interest to an extended-kinship-system-interest beyond an individual 'self-interest' -- and is premised on 'social ethic', mandating the imperative of trusteeship to set apart and to ensure distribution of a pre-determined portion of the proceeds of economic activity to service social needs – to provide for social insurance of the members of the corporation and to build up social capital as *śreṇi dharma* fund. Thus, 'rational self-interest' gets modulated by 'social ethic' imperative of mandatory contributions to the society. It is mandatory because it is the repayment of *ṛṇam* (debt) *śreṇi* owes to the society, because the *śreṇi* gets its unique identity as a legacy from the fore-fathers (*pitṛs*) of *samājam* (society). The 'rational self-interest' gets elevated to self-realization – *ātmajñāna,* elevating the joy of living to ecstasy of being. It is a realization of the ecstasy of being: *yas tu sarvāṇi bhūtāny-ātmany-eva-anupaśyati sarvabhūteṣu ca-ātmānam* (*Īśā Upaniṣad* 6). [trans. 'who sees oneself in all beings and all beings in oneself'.]

The corporate model under capitalism or socialism results in a monopoly entrusted to the state for the legitimate use of force. The consequence is a model of political economy, with a fault-line, which typically survives in many developed states of the world, even today.

This model has the fault-line created by greed leading to impoverishment of many nations and aggrandizement of a few select groups controlling the commanding heights of economies. In the global ethic of *dharma*, no such monopoly was possible. Each village functioned as an independent republic, avoiding the need for the state as an axis between the corporation involved in economic activities and the state operatives' exercise of state power.
It is time to recognize and reinstate *śreṇi dharma*, or social capital, as the missing element of economics to create, nurture and

enhance the wealth of nations, while making *śreṇi dharma* an integral part of modern economic paradigm.

With dharma, yes, we can. We can be the agents of change of the world economy, reaching out to the unreached, endeavoring to achieve the ethical imperative: *sarve bhavantu sukhinah* (let all beings be happy)(ādi śankarācārya).

Those operatives who were to be servants of the people have tried to act like masters denying the very hard-won heritage of freedom and justice.

It is time to reinstate *śreṇi-dharma* (corporate ethic) to combat excessive greed of corporations and state operatives.

Secularism which was an ideological separation of the church and the state has been abused to promote aggrandisement of a chosen few state operatives and corporate honcho's eating into the wealth of the state and of corporations.

Rule of law has been circumvented and often subverted by these greedy people. Even the constitutions which were rules for the organized governance of three estates (executive, legislature and judiciary) limiting state power have been subverted often to hang on to power and pelf. The fourth estate has also become an unregulated, unchecked corporate form with attendant records of abuse and greed. When the fence eats away the field, who is to save the crop? The fourth estate should introspect, revert to and re-assert śreṇi-dharma (corporate ethic).

Dharma is founded on citizens performing their fundamental duties. Performance of fundamental duties is a condition precedent to the enjoyment of their fundamental rights. There has to be a collective re-statement of fundamental duties, foremost of which is the vow to protect dharma, the primordial, eternal, universal ordering principle.

A region which accounted for about 80% of the world GDP (pace Angus Maddison) just three centuries ago can find its rightful place in the comity of nations. This region was impoverished by the action of colonial regimes.

Impoverishment of Colonial Asia

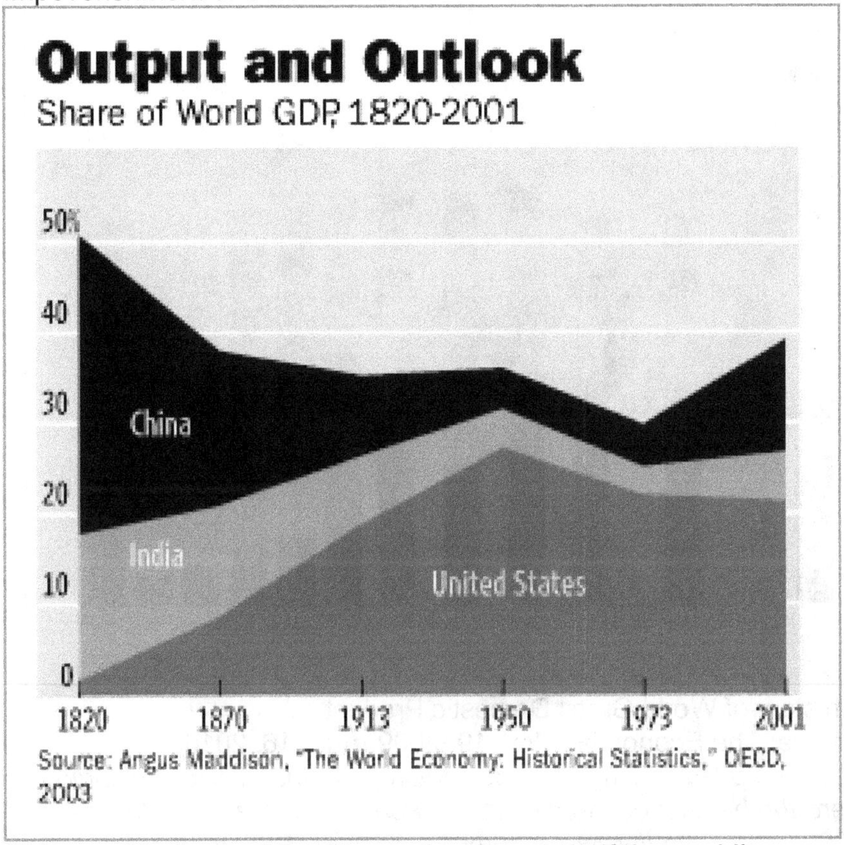

China and India combined to produce nearly half the world's economic output in 1820 compared to just 1.8% for the U.S.

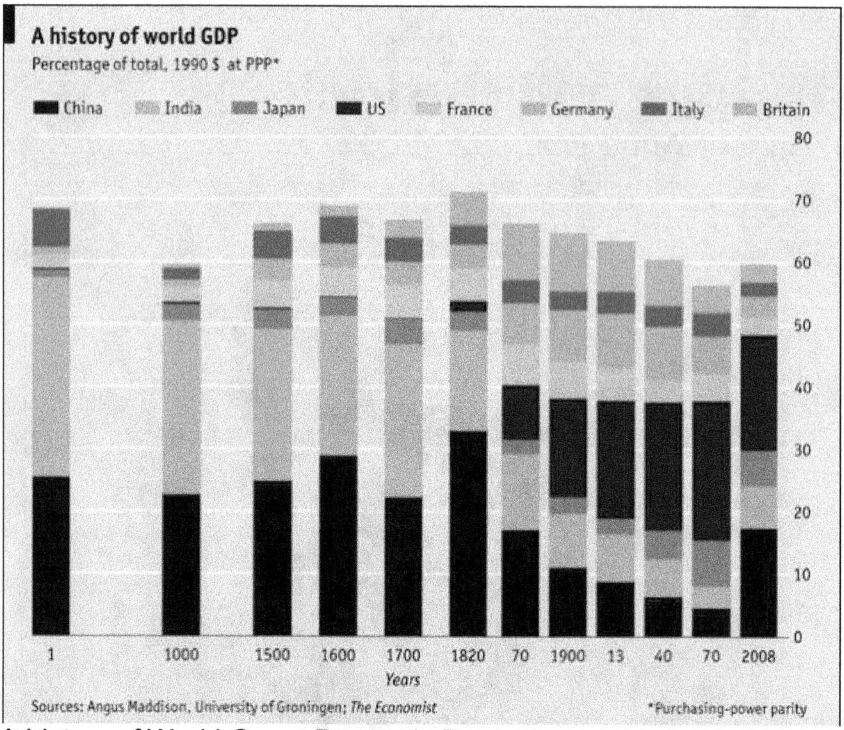

A history of World Gross Domestic Product
Source: The Economist, Nov. 19, 2009, Aug. 16, 2010
Data compiled by Angus Maddison suggest that China and India were the biggest economies in the world for almost all of the past 2000 years. http://www.economist.com/node/16834943
The impoverishment of the two economies with large populations – China and India – resulted in an outrage for dharma finally ending the unjust, adharmic colonial regime. The economies have been trying to catch-up with imperialist dictatorships, ever since the end of the Second World War.

HE FORMED A DIGEST OF HINDU AND MOHAMMEDAN LAWS

Learning dharma at the feet of 'gurus': William Jones, claimed to be 'the (colonial) law-giver of India' is shown wearing a skull-cap on a marble panel from Oxford College chapel. His 'gurus' are shown seated at his feet. This colonial misappropriation of thought has to be exposed.

The financial crisis faced by the developed world requires firm, decisive action to get out of the recession worse than the 1929 depression.

When the world had to reckon with the cost of financing the Second World War, Prime Minister Winston Churchill turned to John Maynard Keynes for an economic framework to prosecute the war. Keynes came up with a brilliant document titled: 'How to Pay for the War (1940)'. This landmark document suggested an economic policy for compulsory saving (essentially wage-earners loaning money to the government), rather than deficit spending, in order to avoid inflation. This measure predicated a substantial increase in the national product, to be effected by a net increase in employment, a longer working day, and a livelier tempo of labor.

A solution analogous to this can be found to overcome the present recessionary market place in the developed world. The formation of an Indian Ocean Community (IOC) will provide a multiplier effect for providing for increase in employment among the 2 billion (1/3rd of the world population) people of the IOC region, while providing an unprecedented opportunity for the developed world to get involved in investing in large projects in the region: Trans-Asian Highway and Trans-Asian Railway from Bangkok to Vladivostok and extending the territorial waters of the Indian Ocean Rim states to 200 nautical miles under the amended Law of the Sea (which has the effect of a marked increased increase, *lebensraum*, for expanding economic opportunities to harness the riches of the ocean).

The rationale for a supra-nation of European Community was initially premised on a Coal and Steel Community but got expanded to full-fledged economic cooperation with Euro as a Common currency and a European Central Bank. This happened as an economic imperative despite the two world wars fought among the European nations. Similarly, IOC can be initiated as a Free Trade Zone, to start with and later to provide for a Common Currency (Mudra) to provide for free movement of goods and services among the 59 states of the Indian Ocean Rim stretching from South Africa to Tasmania along the 63,000 long Indian Ocean Rim.

IOC has a millennium of socio-cultural interaction and bonds which existed among the present-day states of the Indian Ocean Rim. This is exemplified by the statement of the late French epigraphist George Coedes (who wrote about the largest *Viṣṇu* temple of the world in Angkor Wat, Cambodia and other Hindu temples of the Farther Orient) who called the region: Hinduised States of the Farther Orient. The title of his work is: *Histoire ancienne des États hindouisés d'Extrême-Orient*, 1944; translated into English by Hawaii University Press as Indianised States of Southeast Asia). The *'etats hindouises'* is essentially a dharma-dhamma continuum evidenced by thousands of Hindu-Bauddham temples in Malaysia, Indonesia, Thailand, Cambodia, Vietnam, Laos, Burma and other states and historical presence of Hindu kings in the region for over one millennium. The arts, literature and statecraft are substantial replicas of the Indian civilization tradition. When Tagore visited Java, he sang about the golden threads of friendship between India and Indonesia. The Republic Day of 26 Jan. 2011 was graced by the presence of President Susilo Yodhoyono of Indonesia. The opportunities for carrying the cultural bonds into socio-economic spheres of cooperation are immense and have to be seized looking east and by all states supporting the emergence of an economic federation among the Indian Ocean Rim states. The earlier experiences of ASEAN and Asia Pacific Economic Cooperation have to be formalised in an institutional set up as a counterpoise to the European Community. The IOC will be a six trillion dollar GDP powerhouse which can provide for new opportunities for expanded creation of national wealth in the region by providing employment opportunities and integrating the region's finances into the global economic order.

A beginning can be made by expanding the Free Trade Agreements of the type just signed (July 2011) between India and Malaysia to all states of the IOC and by promoting Buddha tourism to India's Buddham pilgrimage centers. The archaeological monuments of the region need to be restored and the priests of the states trained in the performance of traditional festivities and prayers in the Hindu-Bauddha temples of the region. Cultural exchanges in the fields of higher technical education, use of satellite and IT technologies, exchanges among oceanographers will go a long way in strengthening cooperation among the states of IOC.

9 SUSTAINABLE WORLD ORDER

A sustainable world order is a union of federating communities determined to follow the *dharmic* paths.

All identities merge in the identity of life-forms (atman) in a quest to unite with the *paramātman* (supreme divine). All are divine manifestations. All have divinity in them and the potential to achieve nihśreyas, complete bliss in shared welfare.

Social welfare has to be tempered with the responsibility of maintaining a sustainable ecological order. We are mere specks of phenomena in a phenomenological universe and destined to live in harmony with nature.

Corporate and state greed have to be controlled and eradicated.

Social responsibility for creating a sustainable world order demands that all of us should vow to share our wealth with our fellow-human beings and for the sustenance of the natural order. Such sharing has to be preceded by avoidance of excessive consumption which in effect is a denial of a just sharing of the production with our fellow-human beings.

We have to vow to create a world order where we enrich our beings by sharing and by non-violent expressions of outrage against adharma.

Such non-violent outrage is a just crying out for war against injustice, a battle against greed and related corrupt practices, stopping further impoverishment of millions of already impoverished people.

10 *ĀNO BHADRĀH KRATAVO YANTU VIŚWATAH*

(LET NOBLE THOUGHTS COME TO US FROM ALL SIDES)

We are all sparks from the divine anvil.

We are all equally effulgent sparks from the divine anvil.

We are mere instruments in the divine dispensation ordained to protect dharma, the cosmic order.

This sacred tryst with dharma is ours to cherish and pass on to the present and future generations.

Future generations should say of us that we lived for and protected dharma.

There cannot be a greater purpose than this in life.

So, resist injustice and resist inroads into the hard-won freedom.

Let the crying out against adharma be heard loud and clear and echo through all the walls and crevices of the global village.

Let us, together, chant the *Nāsadīya sukta*:

> *Who really knows? Who shall declare it here?*
> *Whence was it born? Whence issued this creation?*
> *Even the divinities came after its emergence.*
> *Then who can tell from whence it came to be?*
> *None knows when creation has arisen;*
> *Whether He made it or did not make it,*
> *He who surveys it in the highest heaven,*
> *Only He knows, or maybe even He knows not.*

As we progress from non-being to being, from being to becoming, we re-enact creation through this *śabda* (utterance) of outrage for dharma.

Together, we pass on the heritage of resistance and non-violent war against adharma.

Peoples' power has to be restored. Seize power for dharma.

Kāla, time, is imperishable. Time is now.

Dharma of our ancestors has protected us. It is now for us to protect dharma and pass on the heritage to present and future generations.

We are living at a time when Vedic River Sarasvati is flowing again from the Great Himalayas. We are living at a time when a resistance movement stopped the destruction of the world heritage monument built in Setusamudram, a bridge called Setubandha or Ramasetu connecting Rameswaram in India and Talaimannar in Sri Lanka – a veritable world heritage monument for dharma.

What made these things succeed was outrage for dharma, remembering the heritage our ancestors have bequeathed to us.

We resisted successfully the onslaughts of wars which took millions of lives.

But, we have failed to organize ourselves into social formations devoid of excessive greed. We have allowed some social formations to oppress the very people whom the formations were supposed to serve with respect and humility.

Monstrosity of greed and arrogance of power should not blind us to the reality that we have the power to shape our lives and our social formations in such a way that the cosmic order, dharma, remains supreme.

We are living in times when the dictatorship of the financial derivatives, options and puts mathematically certified by nerds has become oppressive, preventing the eradication of poverty from the face of the globe.

If we forget, we cease. If we leave outcasts amidst us, we deny humanity.

If we remember, we create and renew our search for knowledge which has given us technological control over phenomena. Let not technological control become a mirage in an unjust world yielding to the greed and dictatorship of financial markets.

Let a wave of non-violent social upheaval shake the world. Let not our children tell us that we left for them an unjust world enmeshed in chaos.

Let our children remember us for restoring order and bequeathing an open society, united in fervor and resolve – an outrage for dharma, a non-violent war against adharma.

Let the fiction of the state become a reality of Rastram for the common good. Let the genitrix who said *aham rāṣṭrī sangamanī*, teach us toddlers to move together, toddling for common welfare.

This can happen when

communities federate into a united Rastram for dharma of, for and by the people living along the waters of the Pacific, Atlantic and Indian Oceans which embrace and toddle the globe.

Sri Rama and Sri Kṛṣṇa are role models in *rājadharma* because they fought two just wars to protect dharma. Their resistance movement to protect dharma, to protest adharma has stood the test of time and has served as a model for many golden pages of struggles for justice and freedom in the history of human civilization.

I quote an excerpt from a speech delivered by Swami Vivekananda on our non-violent, spiritual, sacred mission:

"This is the *puṇya bhūmi*, the land of karma. Today I stand here and say, with the conviction of truth, that it is so. If there is any land on this earth that can lay claim to be the blessed punya bhoomi, to be the land to which souls on this earth must come to account for karma, the land to which every soul that is wending its way towards God must come to attain its last home, the land where humanity has attained its highest towards gentleness, towards generosity, towards purity, towards calmness, above all, the land of introspection and spirituality — it is India". (Lecture delivered in Floral Hall of Colombo, Sri Lanka, on January 16, 1897).

Hindus are now over one billion in number in India alone. They, together with all citizens of the globe, have a destiny to fulfil. To carry the message of dharma rastram to every nook and corner of the globe in all languages.

This selfless endeavor, rendered *l'acte gratuite*, will be a fitting tribute to the memory of that savant, Swami Vivekananda (12 January 1863 – 4 July 1902) who lived for less than 39 years and shone with such brilliance that the sparks of sacred fire of his words pierce even today into every child's being. The global village is too rich a heritage of all of us to be frittered away with fragmented, divisive, intolerant, violent behavior. Mother nature has enough to be shared by everyone on the globe with generosity, purity of heart, and tranquility of atman in an endless quest to understand the *paramātman*, the supreme divine.

Swami Vivekananda on the Platform of the Parliament of Religions 11 September 1893 at the Art Institute of Chicago. Dr. Barrows, the president of the Parliament said, "India, the Mother of religions was represented by Swami Vivekananda, the Orange-monk who exercised the most wonderful influence over his auditors."

Let Rāṣṭram be the path to protect dharma. With the *anugraham* of Devi, of the genitrix mother, everything is possible. She is *rāṣṭrī*, she is the Rāṣṭram. She is the path. With her guidance, toddlers shall walk dharma.

ABOUT THE AUTHOR

Dr. S. Kalyanaraman is Director, Sarasvati Research Center, President, Ramasetu Protection Movement in India and BoD member of World Association for Vedic Studies. His research interests relate to rediscovery of Vedic Sarasvati River, roots of Hindu civilization, decoding of Indus Script, National Water Grid and creation of Indian Ocean Community. He has a Ph.D. in Public Administration from the University of the Philippines. He is a multi-lingual scholar versed in Tamil, Telugu, Kannada, Sanskrit, Hindi. He was a senior financial and IT executive in Asian Development Bank, Manila, Philippines and on Indian Railways. His 18 publications include: *Indian Lexicon* - a multilingual dictionary for over 25 Indian languages, *Sarasvati* in 15 volumes, *Indian Alchemy - Soma in the Veda, Indus Script Cipher, Rastram, Indian Hieroglyphs – Invention of Writing.* He is a recipient of many awards including Vakankar Award (2000), Shivananda Eminent Citizens' Award (2008) and Dr. Hedgewar Prajna Samman (2008). Website: http://sites.google.com/site/kalyan97

www.ingramcontent.com/pod-product-compliance
Lightning Source LLC
Chambersburg PA
CBHW060702280326
41933CB00012B/2271
* 9 7 8 0 9 8 2 8 9 7 1 3 3 *